D1469342

THE FALL CALENDAR COLLECTION

A RESOURCE BOOK FOR K–1 TEACHERS

Leap into the fun of *The Fall Calendar Collection!* Packed full of delightful ideas and activities, this book is sure to brighten up the season by making both special and ordinary days a cause for celebration.

The skills covered in this book are those traditionally taught in the early years of school. Pages are designed to supplement the curriculum needs of lower primary classrooms with a particular emphasis in reading, language arts, math, and art. Some pages offer suggestions or instructions for making classroom aids and activities; other pages are ready to reproduce for immediate student use.

Notice that the pages are perforated and hole-punched for added convenience — organize the pages in file folders or a ring binder, or use and treasure the book as it is.

THE CONTINENTAL PRESS, INC.
Elizabethtown, PA 17022

CONTRIBUTORS

Debbie Diller
Sylvia Foust
Linda Kerlik
Kathy Ringgold
Laurie Williamson

ILLUSTRATORS

Pamela Measley
Sue Sylvester
Jane Via

COVER ARTIST

Don Page

ACKNOWLEDGEMENTS

"Chipmunk" from OUT IN THE DARK AND DAYLIGHT: Poems by Aileen Fisher. Copyright © 1980 by Aileen Fisher. By permission of Harper & Row, Publishers, Inc.

"Creepy" reprinted from INSTRUCTOR, October 1972. Copyright © 1972 by The Instructor Publications, Inc. Used by permission.

"Grizzly Bear" from THE CHILDREN SING IN THE FAR WEST by Mary Austin. Copyright 1928 by Mary Austin. Copyright © renewed 1956 by Kenneth M. Chapman and Mary C. Wheelwright. Reprinted by permission of Houghton Mifflin Company.

"The Scarecrow" from LET'S TAKE A BREAK by Margaret Hillert. Copyright © 1981 The Continental Press, Inc. Reprinted by permission of the author.

ISBN 0-8454-6245-8
Copyright © 1986 The Continental Press, Inc.

Permission is granted, with the purchase of this book, for the individual teacher to reproduce the appropriate pages for use in the classroom. All rights reserved. Printed in the United States of America.

✤ TABLE OF CONTENTS ✤

BULLETIN BOARDS
and LEARNING CENTER ACTIVITIES

BULLETIN BOARDS

LEARNING CENTER ACTIVITIES

This rollicking bulletin board is a cheery welcome to your students as they begin the new school year!

Cover the bulletin board with bright blue corrugated paper. Use cutout letters for the title, or write the title on a white paper cloud. Cut the ladder from gray construction paper and use a long strip of aluminum foil for the slide. Characters are made by cutting circles out of yellow construction paper. Arms and legs are shaped with pipe cleaners and attached in varying positions. Write a child's name on each character; add wide eyes and a big smile!

THE FALL CALENDAR COLLECTION (K–1)
Copyright ©1986 The Continental Press, Inc.

Mrs. Haine's
First Grade
COME IN!

Outside the ☁ may blow
Outside the ❄ may fall
But—
Inside our 😊😊😊 are shining
A happy welcome to all!

Let your class help you make this visitors' welcome board to display on a bulletin board outside your room or on your classroom door.

Have the children draw and color their happiest faces on small paper plates. Attach the faces to a colorful background; add a hearty "WELCOME" sign. Then use a bright piece of poster board for the door. Write the poem on it with bold markers. Shiny aluminum foil provides an eye-catching background for the lettering on the window. Make a doorknob by threading heavy string through the center of a styrofoam ball. Put the string through a small hole in the door and fasten it to a large button on the reverse side. Use staples to attach the door to the background, making sure the "hinge" is strong enough to allow for countless openings.

Keeping your classroom in tiptop shape is a breeze with these two job charts.

Use construction paper for the car, buckets, and children of "The Clean Team." When attaching the bucket cutouts to the bulletin board, bring the sides together slightly to give a three-dimensional effect. Assign jobs by labeling paper towels with children's names and pinning them inside the buckets.

A whimsical bear provides the focal point for "Pumpkin Pie Projects." Make it out of construction paper. For each job, color a paper plate to look like a pumpkin pie. Cut a wedge out of it. Color and divide other plates into six pieces so that there is one wedge for each child in the class. Write student names on the wedge cutouts. Change job assignments by shifting "pie pieces."

THE FALL CALENDAR COLLECTION (K–1)
Copyright ©1986 The Continental Press, Inc.

Apple "Shiners"

Whooo's Been WISE?

These two display boards offer recognition and congratulations to the owners of well-done papers!

To make "Apple Shiners," tack outstanding papers onto big apples cut from red construction paper. Use black and orange paper to create a ladybug. Give the bug a tissue to add extra polish to the already shiny apples!

"Who's Been Wise?" features an owl made from brown and white construction paper. Attach a tree branch to the board for the owl's lookout perch.

THE FALL CALENDAR COLLECTION (K–1)
Copyright ©1986 The Continental Press, Inc.

Go NUTS over LETTERS

Watch your students go nuts over letters with this attractive, fall board!

Cut out acorns from light brown construction paper and caps from green construction paper. Print capital letters on the acorn "bodies." Tack them onto a sprawling, paper oak tree. Securely position a pin above each one. Print matching lowercase letters on the acorn caps. Punch a hole near the top of each cap, making sure the holes are large enough to slip over the pins on the board. Store the caps in an envelope held by the helpful squirrel.

Instruct the children to match the lowercase and capital letters to put the caps on the acorns.

A GAME FOR TWO PLAYERS:

Prepare two sets of acorn caps, using a different shade of green paper for each one. Each player shuffles a set of caps and places them face down in a pile. In turn, each player turns over a cap, identifies the letter, and puts it at the correct place on the board. If a player picks a cap which has already been matched on the board, the cap is simply set aside. It is then the next player's turn. After all matches have been made, each player counts his or her acorn caps on the tree. The player who made the most matches is the winner.

INSTRUCTIONAL BULLETIN BOARD ☆ *Fall*
Matching Capital and Lowercase Letters
*Acorn pattern, page 62
*Certificate acknowledging completion, page 42

9

THE FALL CALENDAR COLLECTION (K–1)
Copyright ©1986 The Continental Press, Inc.

Look who's standing guard over the classroom pumpkin patch!

Make the scarecrow's clothes out of colorful wallpaper samples. Use an old pair of garden gloves for hands, and add yarn or straw for the finishing touches on head and feet. A construction-paper bird provides company for the friendly scarecrow. Children create the pumpkin patch scenes using orange paint, sponges, and markers.

THE FALL CALENDAR COLLECTION (K–1)
Copyright ©1986 The Continental Press, Inc.

Set the stage for an eerie, Halloween scene by tacking a simple, black construction-paper house to a blue background. Add a spindly, brown paper tree beside the house. Put a card key at the bottom of the board. Each card should show a Halloween figure or object and a number from 1 to 9. Make ten cutouts of each item. Store all the cutouts in a plastic pumpkin. Place the pumpkin on a desk or worktable near the board.

Now let the children create the atmosphere! Direct them to pin as many items to the board as the key indicates. Change the key regularly to make the Halloween scene an ever-changing one.

THE FALL CALENDAR COLLECTION (K–1)
Copyright ©1986 The Continental Press, Inc.

Welcome to a Thanksgiving Day celebration! You supply the heading and construction-paper table. Let the children do the rest!

Discuss good table manners with the class. Write suggested good manners on voice balloons. Show the children pictures of the people who were at the first Thanksgiving feast — the Wampanoag Indians, the tribe that lived in the Plymouth area in the early 1600s, and the New England settlers, or Pilgrims. On the chalkboard, list the foods that were eaten at the feast — deer, turkey, geese, clams, oysters, fish, fruits, corn, salads, and maple sugar. Then instruct each child to draw and cut out a Pilgrim or Indian figure (waist up). Encourage children who are finished with their figures early to illustrate the Thanksgiving foods with paper and crayons.

Pin the figures behind the table, sprinkling the voice balloons throughout. Finish by pinning the foods on the table.

BULLETIN BOARD ☆ 🎩
Good Table Manners
*Student participation in construction

12

THE FALL CALENDAR COLLECTION (K–1)
Copyright ©1986 The Continental Press, Inc.

LEAFY LEAP

DIRECTIONS: Take all the leaves and shapes out of the envelope. Put each shape on the correct leaf.

Let this lovable pup motivate your students to dive into shapes! Duplicate or trace the above design. Paste it on the front of a 9" x 12" string-tie envelope. Cut out twelve leaves from colored construction paper. In black, draw an outline of a shape on every leaf (use three different sizes of a circle, square, triangle, and rectangle). Then cut out a felt shape to match the outline on each leaf. Store all the pieces in the envelope.

THE FALL CALENDAR COLLECTION (K–1)
Copyright ©1986 The Continental Press, Inc.

LEARNING CENTER ACTIVITY ☆ *Fall*
Visual Discrimination with Shapes
*Leaf patterns, page 62
*Related worksheet, page 24

13

Use these wacky spiders to weave colorful fun! Cut the web from oaktag. Color the sections as indicated, and secure a small piece of magnetic tape to each one. Then cut out and label eight spiders with color words. For self-checking, put a dot of the appropriate color on the back of each spider. Also, glue a paper clip to the back. Attach a length of heavy string to each spider by threading the yarn through a small hole and knotting it or taping it on the back. In similar fashion, attach the spiders to the web.

THE FALL CALENDAR COLLECTION (K–1)
Copyright ©1986 The Continental Press, Inc.

COUNT! 1-2-3

Let your children practice number concepts in three clever ways!

1 PAPER CLIP CREATURES

Cut creature heads from colorful construction paper. Use markers to draw eyes and a "number nose" on each one. Add pipe cleaner antennae.

Let the children attach paper clips for legs or body parts, making sure each creature has the same number of legs or body parts as the number on its nose.

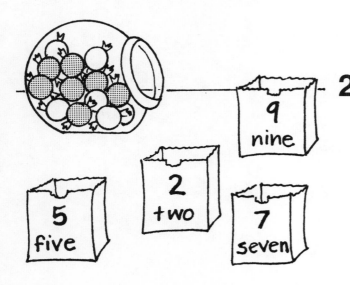

2 TRICKS, NO TREATS!

Label bags with numbers and corresponding number words. Then fill a candy jar with homemade "treats." Small styrofoam balls wrapped with fabric and tied with yarn are great make-believe candies that won't tempt the sweet tooth!

Instruct the children to fill each bag with the correct number of treats.

3 COLORFUL HEADBANDS

Make feather headbands from oaktag strips. Write a number from 1 to 10 on one side of each. Write the matching number word on the other side. Decorate the strips with crayons or markers. Then cut colored feathers from construction paper.

Have the children put the correct number of feathers on each decorated strip (either side) to complete the headband.

Build a SHOPPING CENTER

PAT'S PET SHOP

THE FOOD STORE

CLOTHING MART

TOM'S TOY CENTER

Change a set of poster boards into a shopping center! Simply draw store outlines on the boards and cut them out. Give each store a name. Place the stores with old magazines, scissors, and glue at a worktable.

Now let the children supply the merchandise! Instruct them to cut out things to eat for the grocery store, things to play with for the toy store, things to wear for the clothing store, and types of pets for the pet store. Have the children paste the items on the appropriate stores.

THE FALL CALENDAR COLLECTION (K–1)
Copyright ©1986 The Continental Press, Inc.

WORKSHEETS,
TASK CARDS, and CERTIFICATES

WORKSHEETS

TASK CARDS

CERTIFICATES

Name _____

Color spaces that show **signs of fall** orange .

Be ready to tell what the other pictures make you think of.

THE FALL CALENDAR COLLECTION (K–1)
Copyright ©1986 The Continental Press, Inc.

WORKSHEET ☆ *Fall*
Signs of Fall

18

Name

Help the firefighter put out the fire!
Draw an X on each picture that does not show fire safety.
Color each one that does.

THE FALL CALENDAR COLLECTION (K–1)
Copyright ©1986 The Continental Press, Inc.

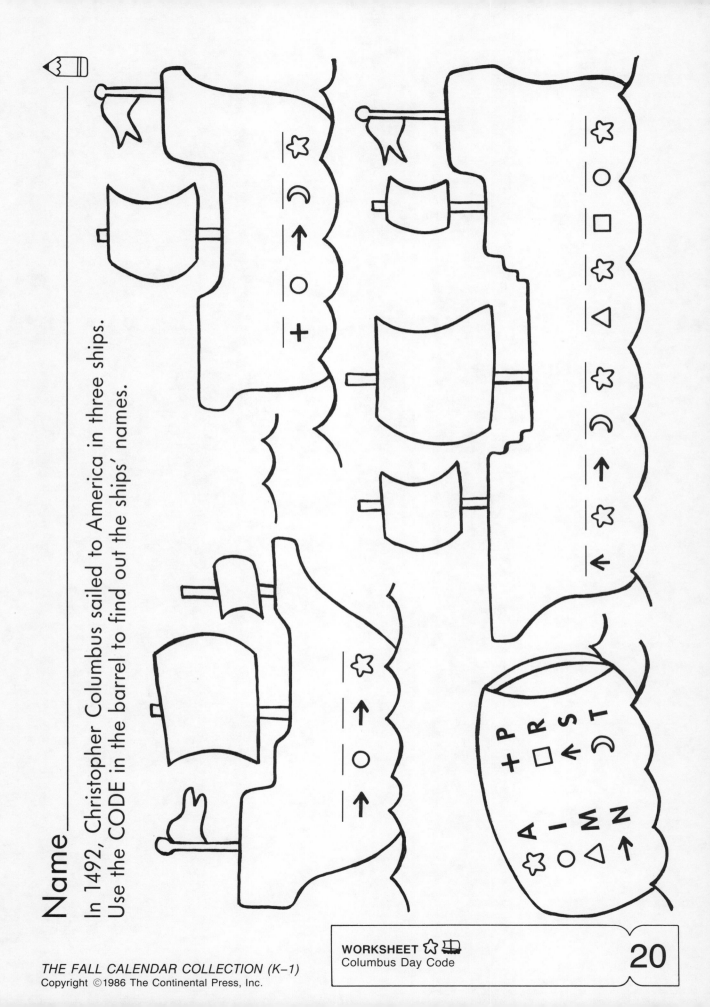

Name _____

In 1492, Christopher Columbus sailed to America in three ships.
Use the CODE in the barrel to find out the ships' names.

THE FALL CALENDAR COLLECTION (K–1)
Copyright ©1986 The Continental Press, Inc.

Name

Halloween eyes are watching YOU!
Color the spaces —

1 orange   **3** blue

2 black   **4** white

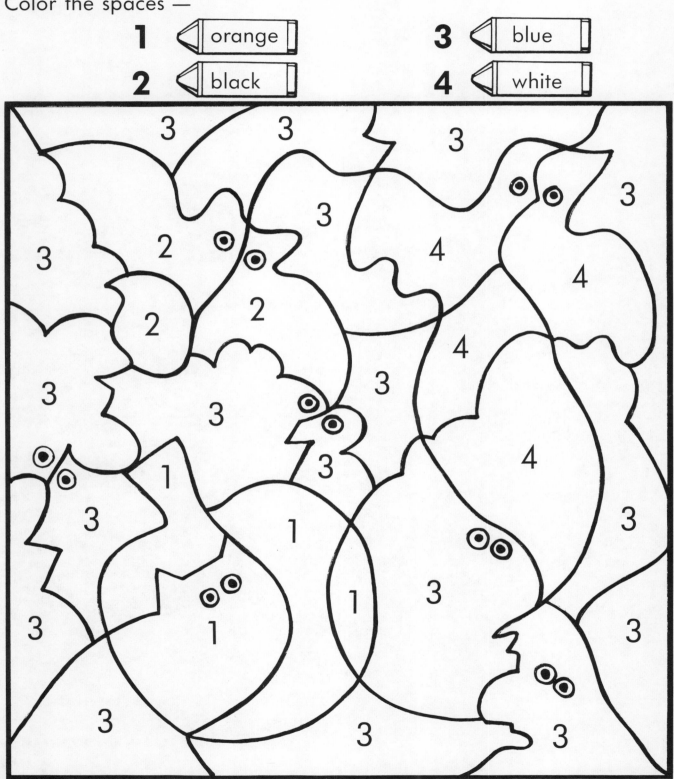

THE FALL CALENDAR COLLECTION (K–1)
Copyright ©1986 The Continental Press, Inc.

Name _____

Color a path from the
Indians to the Pilgrims.

THE FALL CALENDAR COLLECTION (K–1)
Copyright ©1986 The Continental Press, Inc.

WORKSHEET ☆ 🎩
Thanksgiving Day Maze

22

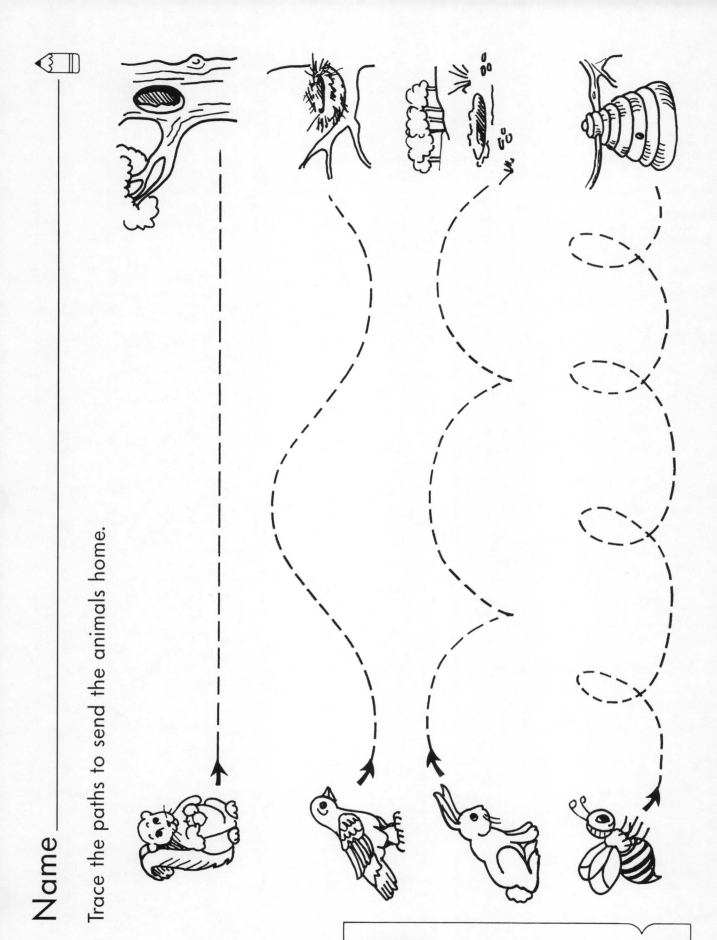

Name _____

Trace the paths to send the animals home.

THE FALL CALENDAR COLLECTION (K-1)
Copyright ©1986 The Continental Press, Inc.

WORKSHEET
Left to Right

23

Name _____

Trace the shapes. Then color the leaves —

circles 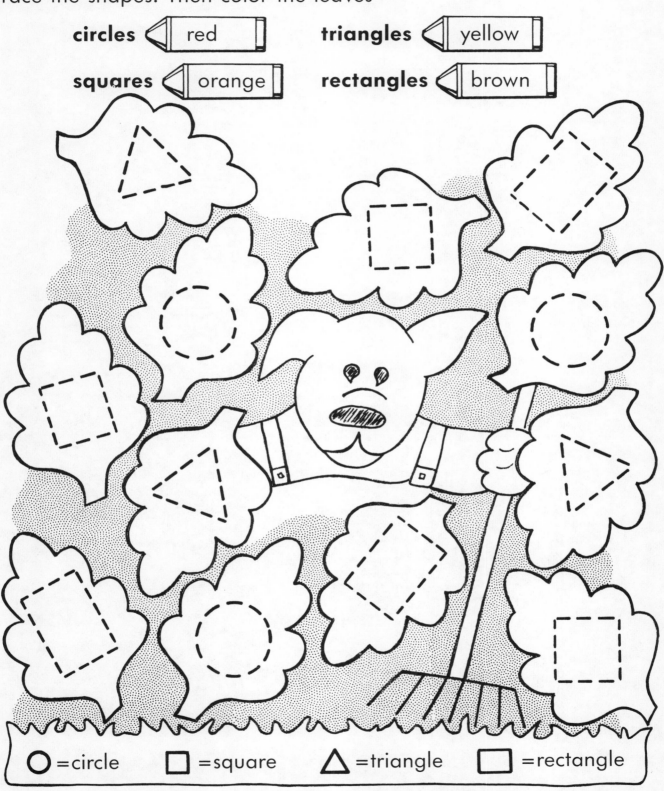 red   **triangles** yellow

squares orange   **rectangles** brown

○ = circle   □ = square   △ = triangle   ▭ = rectangle

THE FALL CALENDAR COLLECTION (K–1)
Copyright ©1986 The Continental Press, Inc.

Name _____

Look at these FANCY FEATHERS!
Cut out the feathers at the bottom of the page.
Paste each one on the turkey feather that matches.
Then color the turkey.

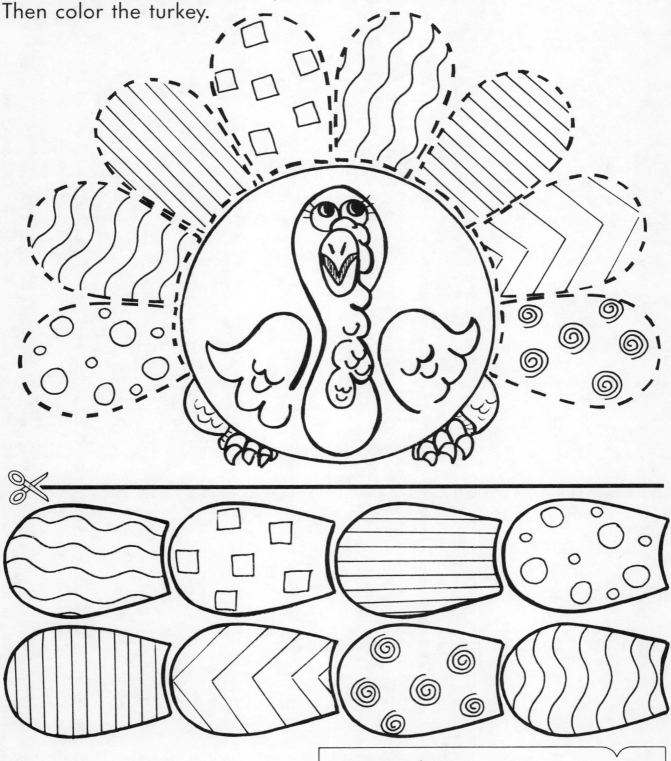

THE FALL CALENDAR COLLECTION (K–1)
Copyright ©1986 The Continental Press, Inc.

Name _____

The sunflower in the box is complete.
Each of the other flowers is missing a part.
Draw the missing part on each flower.
Then color the flowers.

THE FALL CALENDAR COLLECTION (K–1)
Copyright ©1986 The Continental Press, Inc.

Who's nibbling in the garden?
In each group, draw lines to match the animals with the vegetables they like to eat.

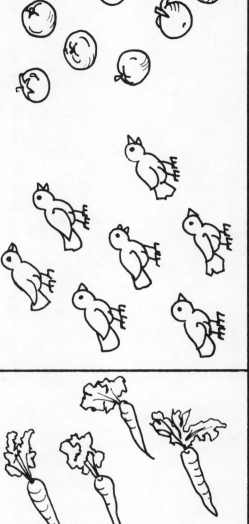

THE FALL CALENDAR COLLECTION (K–1)
Copyright ©1986 The Continental Press, Inc.

Name _____

Old MacDonald had a farm.
E-I-E-I-O!

How many chickens?   How many pigs?

3
_____   _____

Circle the set with **more**.

Yankee Doodle came to town,
A-riding on a pony.

How many feathers?   How many caps?

_____   _____

Circle the set with **less**.

Humpty Dumpty sat on a wall.
Humpty Dumpty had a great fall.

How many horses?   How many men?

_____   _____

Circle the set with **less**.

Baa, baa, black sheep,
Have you any wool?

How many sheep?   How many bags?

_____   _____

Circle the set with **more**.

THE FALL CALENDAR COLLECTION (K–1)
Copyright ©1986 The Continental Press, Inc.

Color the smaller
object in each pair.

Color the larger
object in each pair.

THE FALL CALENDAR COLLECTION (K–1)
Copyright ©1986 The Continental Press, Inc.

Name _____

What WORMY APPLES! Count the worms in each one.
Write the correct number on the line.

| 1 | 2 | 3 | 4 | 5 | 6 | 7 | 8 | 9 |

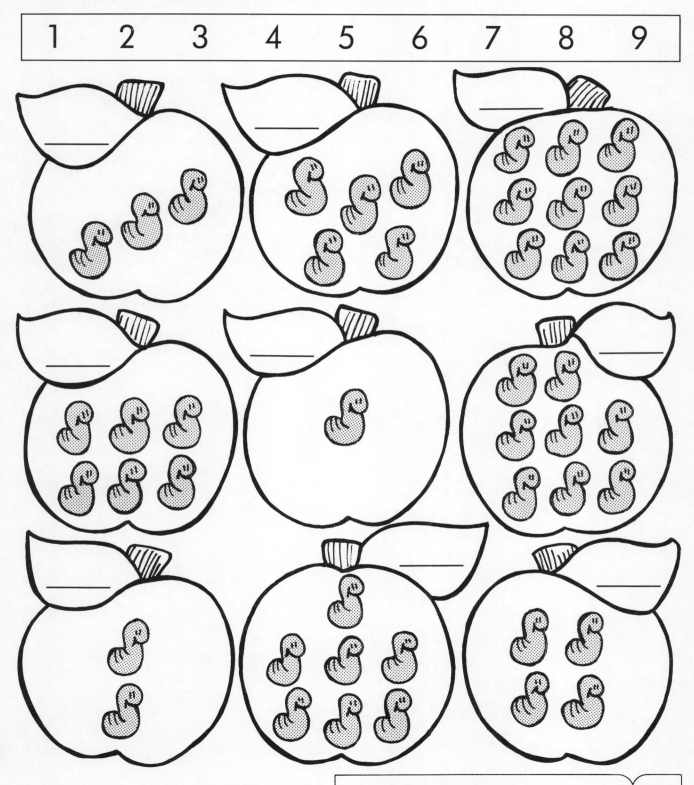

THE FALL CALENDAR COLLECTION (K–1)
Copyright ©1986 The Continental Press, Inc.

Name _____

Use the goodies on each pizza to help you add.
When you are finished, write your name on the
pizza award.

2 +1	4 +1	3 +2
5 +0	1 +3	1 +1
2 +3	0 +2	2 +2

☆ ☆

This certifies that
makes
delicious pizza.

_____

THE FALL CALENDAR COLLECTION (K-1)
Copyright ©1986 The Continental Press, Inc.

Name _____

Who's eating all the popcorn?
Subtract. Write the correct answer in the box.

3
− 1

5
− 4

3
− 2

4
− 2

5
− 3

4
− 3

2
− 1

4
− 1

5
− 2

THE FALL CALENDAR COLLECTION (K-1)
Copyright ©1986 The Continental Press, Inc.

WORKSHEET
Subtraction with Sums to 5

32

Name _____

You can crack these TOUGH NUTS!
Say each pair of picture names.
Color the acorns if the words rhyme.

Name_____

Name the football players!
Say the picture name on each helmet. Write the letter that stands for
the beginning sound on the line. (Use a capital letter, please!)

___am   ___ed   ___at

___ill   ___ary   ___an

___ick   ___en   ___ail

THE FALL CALENDAR COLLECTION (K-1)
Copyright ©1986 The Continental Press, Inc.

Name _____

After the turkey's been eaten, make a wish on me!
Connect the dots from A to Z.
Then draw and color a picture of something you are wishing for on the
  back of this paper.

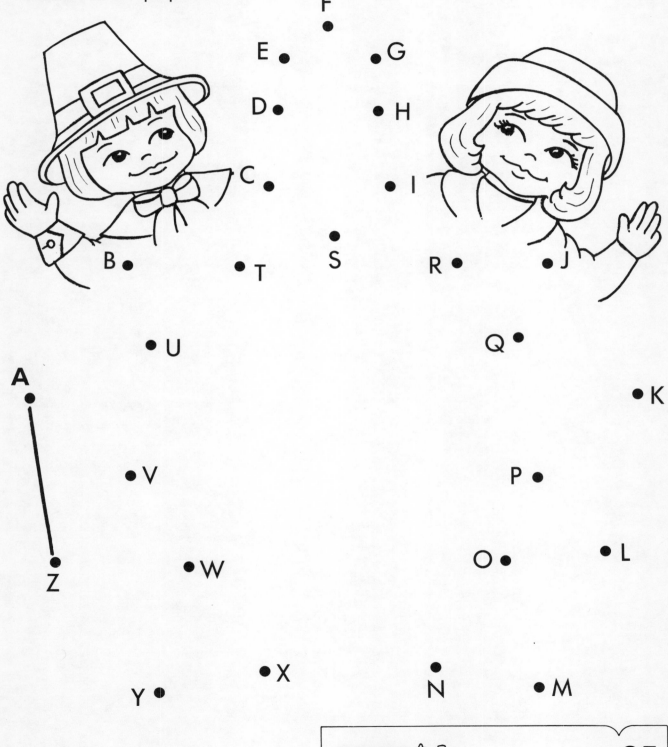

THE FALL CALENDAR COLLECTION (K–1)
Copyright ©1986 The Continental Press, Inc.

Name_____

Draw a line to match each object with the person who would use it.
Then color the pictures.

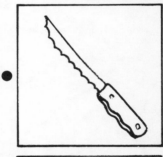

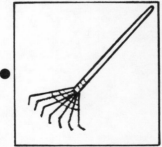

WORKSHEET ☆ *Fall*
Picture Associations

36

THE FALL CALENDAR COLLECTION (K–1)
Copyright ©1986 The Continental Press, Inc.

Name

Cut out the pictures at the bottom of the page.
Paste them in the boxes to show the steps in making a jack-o'-lantern.

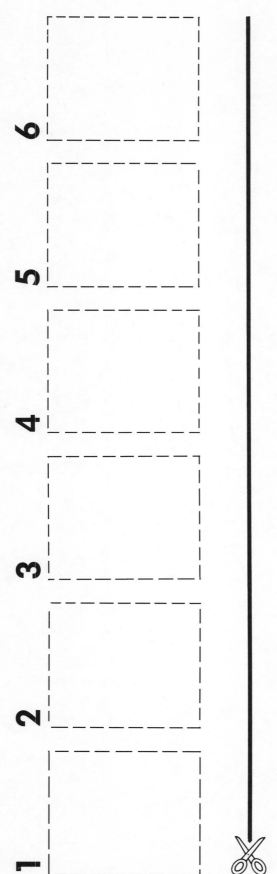

1 **2** **3** **4** **5** **6**

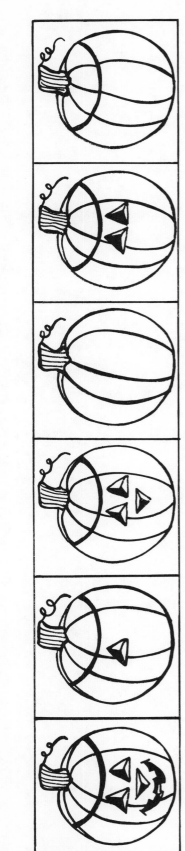

THE FALL CALENDAR COLLECTION (K–1)
Copyright ©1986 The Continental Press, Inc.

Name _____

Listen as your teacher reads "The Gingerbread Boy."
Then cut out the puzzle pieces below.
Put the pieces together to show a picture of the Gingerbread Boy.
Paste the picture on another sheet of paper.
Then color the Gingerbread Boy DELICIOUS!

Three Wishes

The GREAT PUMPKIN has granted you three wishes.
Draw three things you wish for on a piece of paper.

Mirror! Mirror! On The Wall

What are you wearing today? Draw a picture of yourself wearing the clothes you have on. Don't forget to put a smile on your face!

THE FALL CALENDAR COLLECTION (K–1)
Copyright ©1986 The Continental Press, Inc.

Letter and Number Art

Get a piece of  and some .
Draw a big letter or number on the .
Make it into something.

EXAMPLES:

Toothpick Fun

Get a bunch of toothpicks.
Put them on your desk to look like —

1.

2.

3.

4.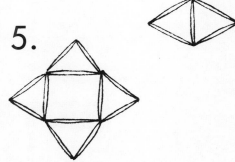

5.

✱ Now make some designs of your own.

THE FALL CALENDAR COLLECTION (K–1)
Copyright ©1986 The Continental Press, Inc.

Happy Birthday to YOU!

Name _____

Date _____

Draw candles on the cake to show how old you are.

I CAN COUNT TO 10!

Name _____

Date _____

NEAT WORK AWARD

Given to _____

On _____

By _____

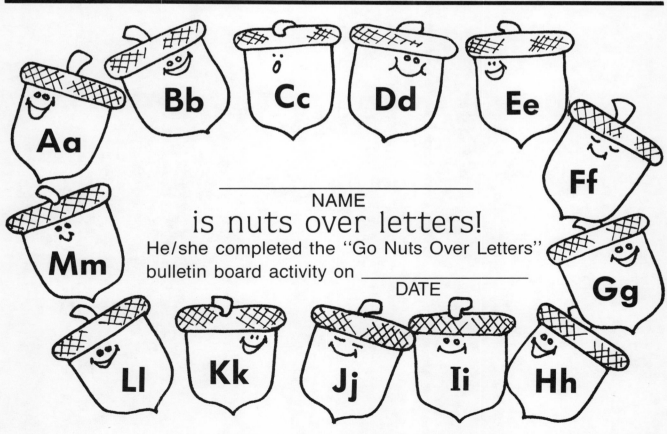

Aa Bb Cc Dd Ee Ff

_____
NAME
is nuts over letters!
He/she completed the "Go Nuts Over Letters"
bulletin board activity on _____
DATE

Mm Gg

Ll Kk Jj Ii Hh

THE FALL CALENDAR COLLECTION (K–1)
Copyright ©1986 The Continental Press, Inc.

POEMS and RELATED ACTIVITIES

The Scarecrow

— *by Margaret Hillert*

The scarecrow stands in the field all day

Scaring the big black crows away.

"Caw, caw, caw."

He doesn't scare <u>me</u>, for all the while

He wears a great big painted smile.

"Haw, haw, haw."

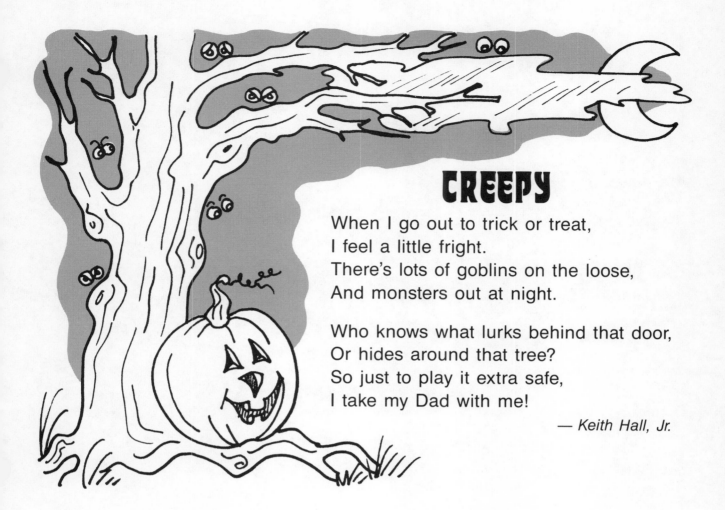

CREEPY

When I go out to trick or treat,
I feel a little fright.
There's lots of goblins on the loose,
And monsters out at night.

Who knows what lurks behind that door,
Or hides around that tree?
So just to play it extra safe,
I take my Dad with me!

— Keith Hall, Jr.

Remember these trick or treating safety tips:

- Buy flameproof costumes only. If your costume is made at home, make sure the fabric is treated with a flame-resistant solution.
- Instead of putting a mask or costume over your face, use makeup. If your costume must be worn over your head, make sure the eye holes are large enough to allow clear vision.
- Wear white or use reflective tape on your costume or goodie bag. That will help make sure that motorists see you.
- If your costume calls for a broom, sword, wand, etc., make it out of cardboard. Sharp objects can be dangerous.
- Go trick or treating with an adult or older friend.
- Walk on lighted streets only and carry a flashlight.
- Stop only at houses of people you know.
- Never accept rides from strangers.
- When you get home, let Mom or Dad check your treats before you eat them.

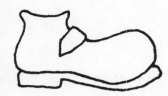

One, two,
Buckle my shoe;

Three, four,
Knock at the door;

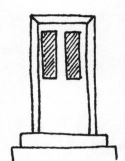

Five, six,
Pick up sticks;

Seven, eight,
Lay them straight;

Nine, ten,
A good fat hen.

Read the Mother Goose rhyme.
Then do these things —

• Draw a 🏠 on the 👟 .

• Draw a ⭕ on the 🚪 .

• Draw two ✕ in the 🌿 .

• Draw three ⬭ under the 🐓 .

THE FALL CALENDAR COLLECTION (K–1)
Copyright ©1986 The Continental Press, Inc.

POEM
Mother Goose Rhyme
Following Directions Activity

46

Name

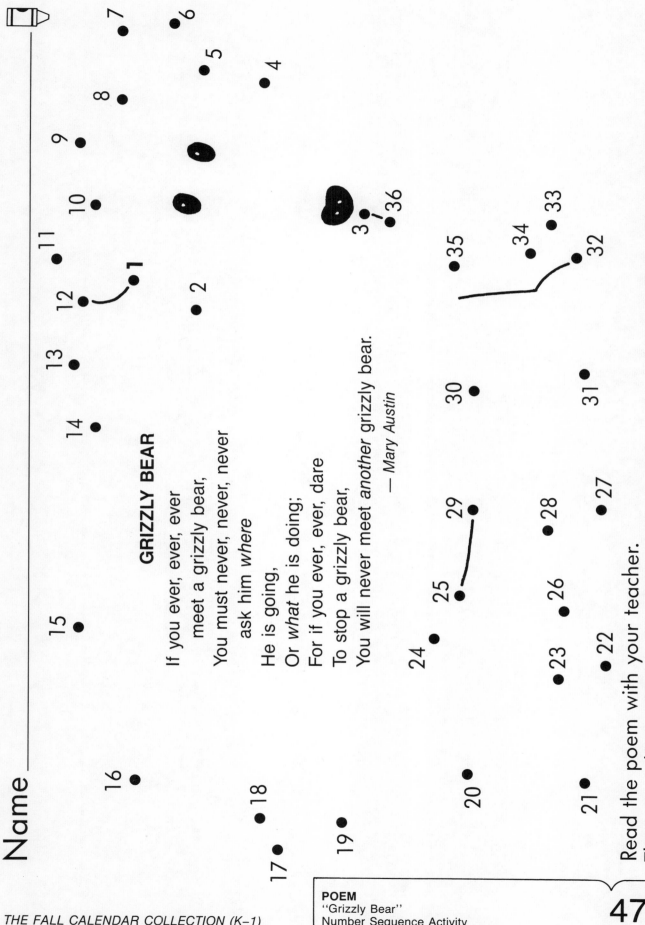

GRIZZLY BEAR

If you ever, ever, ever
meet a grizzly bear,
You must never, never, never
ask him *where*

He is going,
Or *what* he is doing;
For if you ever, ever, dare
To stop a grizzly bear,
You will never meet *another* grizzly bear.

— *Mary Austin*

Read the poem with your teacher.
Then use a <u>brown</u> crayon to connect the dots from 1 to 36. BEWARE OF THE BEAR!

THE FALL CALENDAR COLLECTION (K–1)
Copyright ©1986 The Continental Press, Inc.

POEM
''Grizzly Bear''
Number Sequence Activity

47

CHIPMUNK

I saw a little chipmunk
scamper through the hay,
up a log, and down a log,
and over and away.

I tried my best to follow,
to look at him once more,
but he went home a secret way
and used his secret door.

— Aileen Fisher

Read the poem with your teacher.
Then color the spaces:

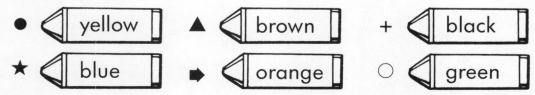

● yellow ▲ brown + black

★ blue ➡ orange ○ green

POEM
"Chipmunk"
Coloring Fun Activity

48

THE FALL CALENDAR COLLECTION (K–1)
Copyright ©1986 The Continental Press, Inc.

GAMES and
CLASSROOM ACTIVITIES

Name that SOUND!

Cut out and paste, or draw pictures of objects on sheets of white paper. Use objects whose names begin with true consonant sounds (see box on right for "fall" suggestions). You will need half as many pictures as children in your class. Then make two small construction-paper cards for each picture. Write the letter that stands for the beginning sound of the picture name on the cards.

bus	moon
desk	notebook
football	pencil
garden	rake
helmet	teacher
jacket	wagon
leaf	yo-yo

Have the children sit in a circle. Give each student a letter card (two students should have the same letter). Instruct the children to lay the cards face up in front of them. Then hold up one picture card. The students with the cards that show the correct beginning letter stand up and run counterclockwise around the circle before returning to their original seats. The first child to be seated and quiet is the winner. Repeat the procedure with a new picture card. After several times, let the children switch letter cards. Then play some more.

VARIATIONS: Have children listen for final consonant sounds.
           Use holiday pictures.

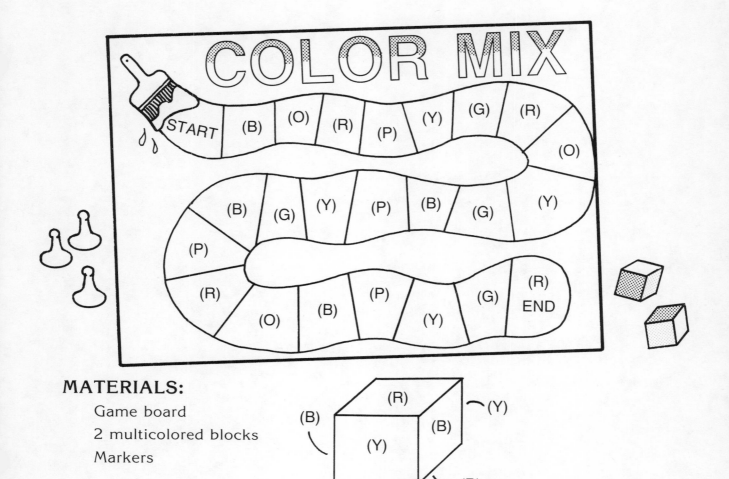

MATERIALS:

Game board

2 multicolored blocks

Markers

*Draw the game board on a large, white poster board. Color the sections as indicated (B – blue, R – red, Y – yellow, G – green, P – purple, O – orange). Use construction paper or paint to color the sides of two blocks (see diagram above), or make a pair of homemade dice and color them appropriately.

HOW TO PLAY:

1. Two or three players each place a marker on START.

2. In turn, each player "rolls the blocks." If the two colors shown on the blocks are the same, the player moves his or her marker to the next same-colored space on the board. If the colors on the blocks are different, the player must decide what color would be made by mixing the two colors (e.g., blue and red — purple). The player then moves his or her marker to the next space of that color on the board.

3. The first person to reach END is the winner.

THE FALL CALENDAR COLLECTION (K–1)
Copyright ©1986 The Continental Press, Inc.

GAME
Color Blending
*Die pattern, page 64
*Designed for 2–3 players

51

Color the Jack·o·Lantern!

MATERIALS:

Game sheet for each player

Homemade die

Crayons

Markers

*Duplicate a stack of game sheets so the game can be played over and over again. Make a homemade die that shows only 1s, 2s, and 3s. Use old game pieces or different-colored buttons as markers.

HOW TO PLAY:

1. Two or three players each start with a game sheet and a pack of crayons. Each player places a marker on his or her sheet at START. One die is shared by both players.

2. In turn, each player rolls the die and moves the marker the correct number of spaces on the game sheet. He or she then follows the directions shown on the board. If the block is empty, nothing needs to be done.

3. The players continue to move around and around the game sheet until one player completely colors his or her pumpkin and is proclaimed the winner.

GAME ☆ ☺
*Game sheet, page 53
*Die pattern, page 64
*Designed for 2–3 players

52

THE FALL CALENDAR COLLECTION (K–1)
Copyright ©1986 The Continental Press, Inc.

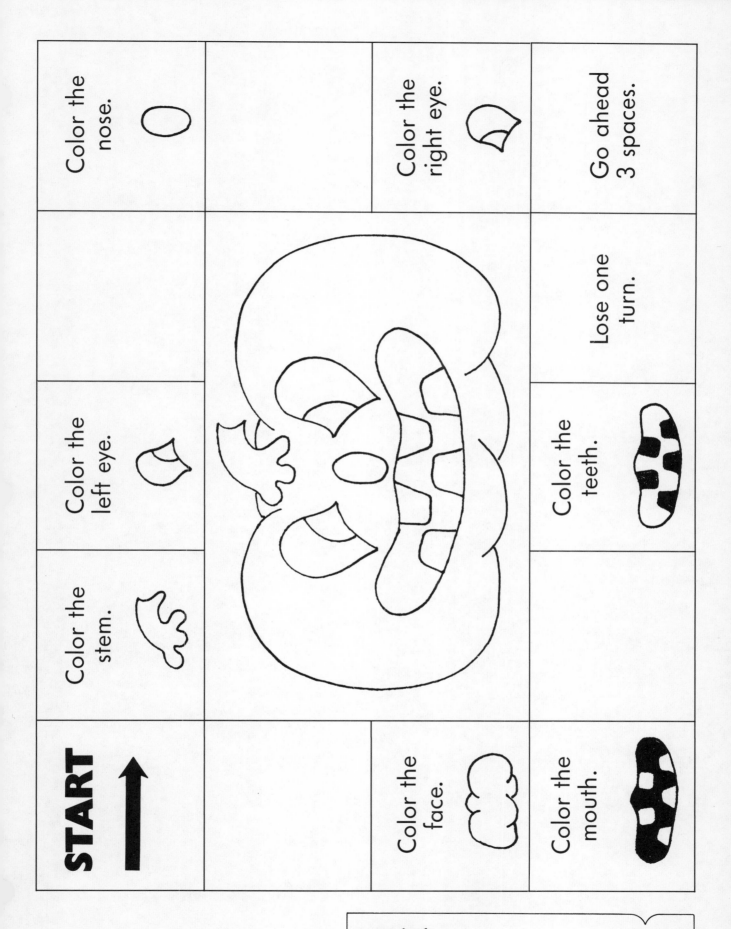

Color the nose.

Color the right eye.

Go ahead 3 spaces.

Lose one turn.

Color the left eye.

Color the stem.

Color the teeth.

START

Color the face.

Color the mouth.

Thanksgiving Visit

MATERIALS:

Game board
Game cards
Markers

*Draw the game board on a large poster board. Make a set of game cards out of oaktag. Write a number from 0 to 5 on most of the cards. On the other cards, write phrases to match those on the game board. Use old game pieces or different-colored buttons as markers.

HOW TO PLAY:

1. Two or three players each place a marker on MY HOUSE. Cards should be shuffled and placed face down on a pile.

2. In turn, each player picks a card. If the card shows a number, the player moves his or her marker ahead that number of spaces. If the card shows a phrase, the marker should be moved to the space on the board with matching words. The card should then be placed back in the pile.

3. The first player to reach GRANDFATHER'S HOUSE is the winner.

CALENDAR COVER-UPS

APPLE TREATS

Let every day in September bring a special "something-to-do" treat. Make a brown, construction-paper apple tree. Hang it near your September calendar. Cut out thirty apples from red construction paper. Number the apples from 1 to 30. On the back of each one, write a task that the class can do together (e.g., Sing a song. Play Simon Says. Name five red things. Count to 20). Pin the apples to the tree with the numbers facing out. Daily, remove the cutout showing the day's date. Join the class in doing the activity written on the back. Then pin the apple to the correct block on the calendar.

AN OCTOBER HOUSEFUL

Change your October calendar into a haunted house. Use construction paper for the black roof, brown tree, and yellow moon. The web can be made from white string or netting. Then cut out thirty-one figures from colored construction paper. Number the figures from 1 to 31. At the start of each day, pin the figure showing the day's date to the correct "window" of the house. You and your students will delight to see the house fill with haunting cutouts as the witching hour of Halloween approaches.

NOVEMBER COUNTDOWN

This colorful wall decoration used in conjunction with the November calendar will give your students something to "talk turkey" about! Make the turkey out of brown poster board. Cut out thirty circles from brightly colored construction paper. After numbering the circles from 1 to 30, tape or pin them to the turkey. Daily, remove the circle showing the day's date. Pin it to the correct block on the calendar. Replace the circle taken from the turkey with a crepe-paper feather. Start with a circle of crepe paper. Press a pencil, eraser-end down, into the center of it. Pull the paper up around the pencil. Then press the center of the circle into a dot of glue and onto the turkey.

LET'S MOVE!

PLAY FOOTBALL

Have the children listen carefully as you read the story below. Discuss any words which may be unfamiliar to the students. Then reread the story, this time encouraging the children to close their eyes and picture the actions in their minds. Next have the class move to a large, open area. Once again, read the story. Pause after each sentence, giving the children plenty of time to perform the action.

> Find your own self space. Pretend you are on a football field. Pick up the football. Feel its shape and the bumpy brown leather. It's kickoff time. Kick the ball into the air. Watch it soar. It's down on the 10-yard line. Dive on it. Stand up again. Toss the ball. Now be the receiver, and catch the ball. There is your goalpost (point to one end of the area). Hold the ball under your arm and run for a touchdown. Now be a cheerleader. Jump up and down and yell for your team. (Blow a whistle.) OK, team, it's halftime. Sue (choose a child) is the quarterback. Get in a straight line behind her. Follow her to the locker room (point to one side of the area). When you get there, have a seat on the bench.

FALLING LEAVES

Give each child a crepe-paper streamer. Use the colors of fall leaves — red, yellow, orange, brown, and green. Instruct the children to spread out over a large, open area. Then try these activities.

1. How many ways can you move your streamer in your self space? Move around the whole area. How many ways can you make it move now?

2. Pretend your streamer is a fall leaf. Make it move on a breezy day, a calm day, a gusty day, a stormy day.

3. Someone is raking the leaves into a large pile (all move to the center of the area with their streamers). Someone has jumped into the pile. The wind blows and scatters the leaves everywhere!

4. All the leaves are dancing in the wind. Freeze. Now only the red leaves are dancing. Freeze. Now green and yellow leaves are twirling in the wind. . .

ART PROJECTS
and PATTERNS

SMOKEY BEAR

PAPER BAG PUPPET

Let your children make "talking" Smokey Bears to remind them to be careful with fire.

MATERIALS:
Each child needs —
Smokey Bear cutout sheet
Standard size lunch bag
Scissors
Crayons
Glue

PROCEDURE:
Give each child the materials listed above. Instruct the children to color and cut out Smokey Bear's head, arms, and boots. Then have them paste the pieces on lunch bags, making sure the heads are pasted on the flaps of the bags. Let the children complete their Smokey Bear puppets by coloring pairs of blue overalls on the bags.

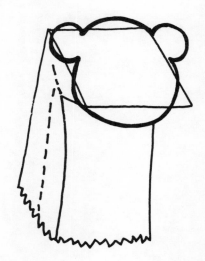

THE FALL CALENDAR COLLECTION (K–1)
Copyright ©1986 The Continental Press, Inc.

SMOKEY

ART PROJECT
Paper Bag Puppet
Instructions for construction, page 58

59

STATUE OF LIBERTY DESK TOP HOLDER

October 28 is the Statue of Liberty's "birthday." On that date in 1886, President Grover Cleveland dedicated the monument which stands on Liberty Island in New York Harbor. Let your students celebrate the occasion by making desk top holders for crayons, pencils, erasers, scissors, etc.

MATERIALS:

Each child needs —

6 oz. milk carton (top opened and straightened up)

12" x 4" piece of tan construction paper

6" x 6" piece of green construction paper

Statue of Liberty cutout (reproduced on gray construction paper)

Scissors

Crayons

Glue

PROCEDURE:

Give each child the materials listed above. Instruct the class to draw lines on the tan paper to make it look like a brick wall. Then glue should be put on the back of the paper, and the "brick wall" folded around the milk carton. Next, have each child trim the corners of the green paper and use crayons to add a grassy texture. After glue has been applied to the bottom of the carton, the carton should be attached to the center of the green paper. Finally, the Statue of Liberty should be cut out. Glue should be put on the back near the bottom, and the statue attached to an inside wall of the carton.

ART PROJECT
Desk Top Holder
Statue of Liberty pattern, page 64

60

SPONGE Pumpkin Prints

(Art Idea by Pat Hornafius)

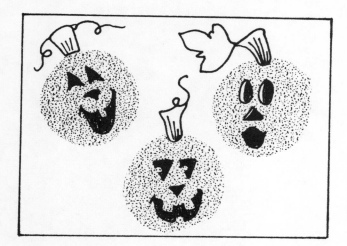

MATERIALS:

Each child needs —

- 9″ x 12″ sheet of white construction paper
- 4″ x 6″ piece of paper for stencil
- Small square of sponge
- Orange tempera paint
- Scissors
- Pencil
- Black marker
- Green crayon

*In addition, newspaper is needed to cover the tables or desks, and paper plates are needed to hold the orange paint.

PROCEDURE:

First, cover all work areas with newspaper. Put small amounts of orange tempera paint on paper plates and place the plates at central locations on tables or groups of desks. Give each child the materials that are listed above.

Direct the students in making the pumpkin stencils — "Hold the piece of 4″ x 6″ paper the short way. Fold it in half. Now place two fingers at the top of the stencil. Make a pencil dot on the fold right under them. Do the same at the bottom, putting the pencil dot above the fingers. Place three fingers on the cut side of the paper and put the pencil dot beside them. Next use a pencil to connect the dots. Starting at the fold, cut along the pencil lines. Throw away the paper that falls out. The remaining paper is the stencil."

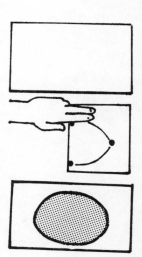

Next demonstrate to the children how to print the pumpkins using the stencil, sponge, and paint before allowing them to print on their own. To demonstrate, place the stencil on the white paper. Using a small amount of paint on the sponge, paint around the outside of the pumpkin first. Then fill in the center, pressing very lightly on the sponge. (It is wise to blot the sponge on the newspaper before printing to rid the sponge of excess paint.) Allow a few minutes for the paint to dry. Then print more pumpkins, one at a time.

After the children have finished printing, and the pictures have had a few minutes to dry, instruct the students to make faces on their pumpkins with black markers, and pumpkin leaves and tendrils with green crayons.

VARIATION: Have the children create trick-or-treat bags by printing their designs on paper bags.

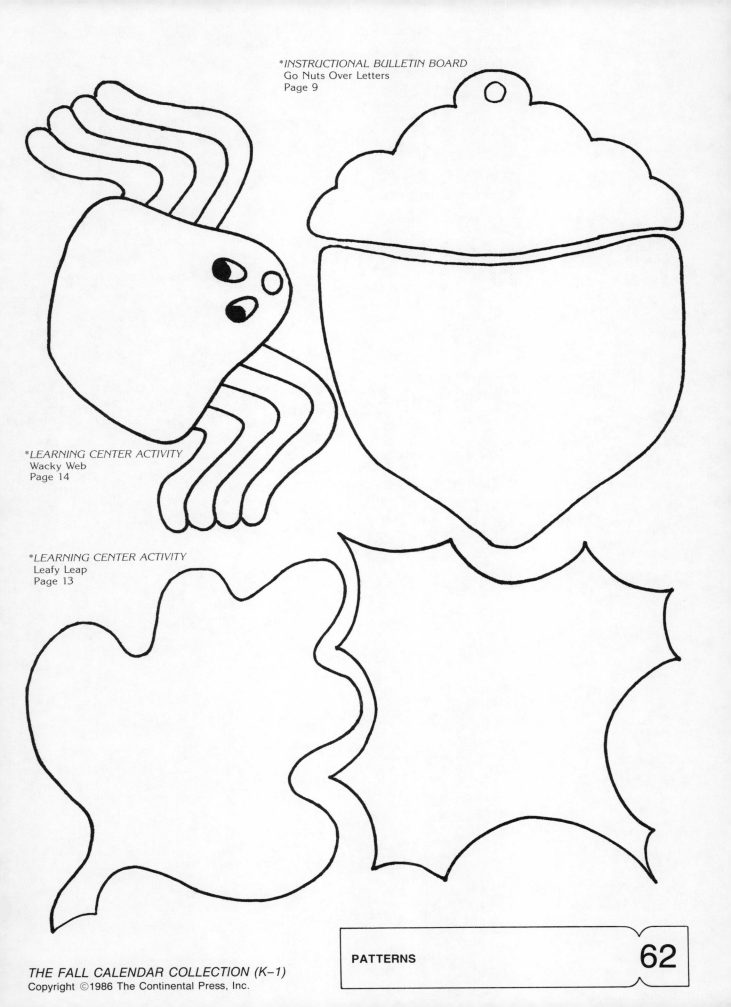

*INSTRUCTIONAL BULLETIN BOARD
Go Nuts Over Letters
Page 9

*LEARNING CENTER ACTIVITY
Wacky Web
Page 14

*LEARNING CENTER ACTIVITY
Leafy Leap
Page 13

PATTERNS

62

THE FALL CALENDAR COLLECTION (K–1)
Copyright ©1986 The Continental Press, Inc.

THE FALL CALENDAR COLLECTION (K–1)
Copyright ©1986 The Continental Press, Inc.

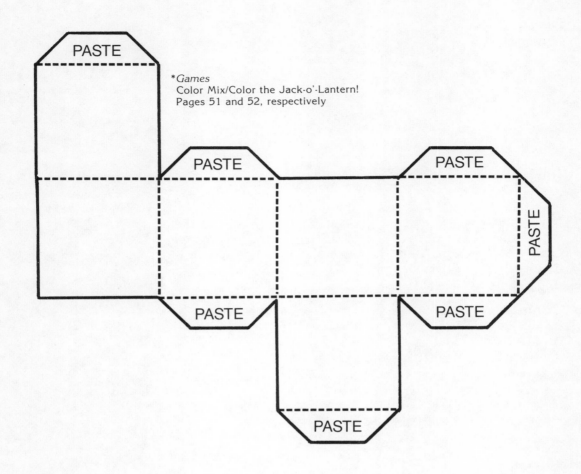

PASTE

*Games
Color Mix/Color the Jack-o'-Lantern!
Pages 51 and 52, respectively

PASTE

PASTE

PASTE

PASTE

PASTE

PASTE

*ART PROJECT
Statue of Liberty Desk Top Holder
Page 60

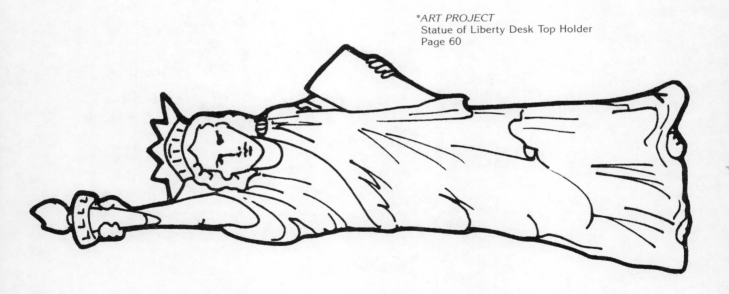

PATTERNS

64

THE FALL CALENDAR COLLECTION (K–1)
Copyright ©1986 The Continental Press, Inc.